Learning To Survive

Learning To Survive

By

V. S. Brynn

About the Book

Learning To Survive is a must-read work for anyone touched by cancer. It also provides an important perspective for those trying to prevent the disease. It is not a typical cancer story. Packed with survival tips, innovative ideas, and strategies for dealing with cancer, this book examines the whole process. It begins with the shock of diagnosis; the need to make decisions; treatment information; and ends with a valuable resource list. Included also are a discussion of support and nutritional options. All individuals concerned about their health could benefit from this book.

The author had an advanced case of breast cancer and she wants to share what she has learned about surviving. Recently diagnosed patients should find the work to be of great comfort and use. The book offers friends and families of cancer patients an easily comprehensible overview of having the illness; several autobiographical accounts are included. For those in the medical profession, who wish to understand the impact of a cancer diagnosis on a patient, this book is for you.

With a light, informative tone, Learning To Survive maintains that survival is a skill and that it can be learned. It is an inspirational look at how to stay alive. Instead of being a medical text, it's a quick-read, witty communication of vital facts and hope for everyone.

Chapter I

Diagnosis: Breast Cancer

Prior to having cancer, I thought of survival as a wilderness skill. Images of Alaskan mountains popped into my head. I pictured a sole traveler, half frost-bitten, clinging to life as he faced grizzly bears and other threats, miles from civilization. The brave wanderer would be found or saved within minutes of disaster. Mankind often succeeded over seemingly insurmountable obstacles. I suppose that the sort of survival I'd previously envisioned was a primal instinct. The type of survival I'm learning about is also a skill.

Can survival be taught? Is it similar to studying French? If operating from the premise that survival is a skill, then why couldn't we learn the necessary techniques?

Cancer causes some of us to embark upon a journey of self-discovery, anyway. Our thought processes can assist or hinder us on the path toward healing. In order to cope with cancer, I tried to study methods which might help me achieve my goal of survival. To paraphrase Woody Allen: "I don't want to attain immortality through my work. I want to attain immortality through not dying."

How should I explain what it meant to go from a happy, healthy, woman to a breast cancer patient? My life literally changed overnight. I've wrestled with whether or not to relive those days through this writing. If it's possible to derive one idea from my story which will help, then it will be worth it. What follows are not medical recommendations, but a description of the wild journey I've taken "Through the Looking Glass" into another world. Although I'm still in a high-risk category for a recurrence, as of this moment, I'm hoping to survive.

I was in my forties, a contented mom of three fantastic kids, happily married, and we were the new owners of a home we were all enjoying. There was some stress surrounding the move and our old house hadn't sold yet. We were settling into our new existence in the spring of 1996. The beauty of the region was impressive and the weather was mild. The countryside was an adventure. We had groundhogs and deer in the backyard; the birdlife was varied and amazing. Having only been in urban or suburban environments in the past, the sight of turtles laying eggs was still a novelty.

Sometime in February of 1996, I'd noticed a "hardness" in one breast just before my period was due. It was not a defined lump, but simply a feeling that was different. I was careful to have annual pap smears and my mammograms were scheduled about two years apart. Without any history of serious illness, I'd been a fortunate female. Not being prone to over-reacting, I'd mentioned to my husband that, instead of tenderness, my left breast seemed "harder" for about a day. We concluded that it was a normal, pre-menopausal type situation and I checked my breasts for lumps. In the business of everyday life, the matter went to the back of my mind and didn't resurface until after a relative's visit. My breast felt hard again in April. This time, by pushing against the breast, I thought I could feel something there, too. The problem was that it was not a clearly outlined lump, but I became nervous.

I usually had my gynecological check-up in the summer. Since it was April, I decided to call and have the breast looked at for an opinion. I told myself it was most likely a cyst and not to panic. We have a few medical guides in the house so I ended up browsing through them. One paragraph jumped out at me: If there is a change in symmetry in the breasts, it could be a sign of breast cancer. The nipples should be checked as well. I immediately ran to a mirror. In the new home, we didn't have a mirror placed where I saw my reflection after showering. It had been some time since I'd really looked at my own breasts. Sure enough, the left one didn't seem symmetrical with the right!

My gynecologist happens to be the obstetrician who delivered two of my three kids. A kind-hearted guy, he said that I could come right in to see him; he added that I probably had a cyst and he'd try to aspirate it. He knew that I'd breast fed my children for a year each and that they were born through "natural childbirth" without complications. He regarded me as a healthy mom. I didn't smoke and my vices were few. An occasional coffee, glass of wine, or chocolate bar were consumed, but my diet was truly an example of everything in moderation.

The nightmare began when the aspiration needle came up dry. Now the doctor and his assistant looked concerned. "I know a surgeon who could take a look at this..."

I was a mess. "What do you think it is?"

Thanks to my doctor's understanding, a surgeon was lined up quickly. I soon found myself undergoing another attempt at aspirating "something." No one could really feel an entire lump, but they could touch a hard spot that seemed to be deep in the breast. The surgeon, an older fellow from South America with a paternal air, calmly suggested that we try an ultrasound. Still nothing. The surgeon's office happened to be in a "Breast Center," complete with an imaging business. Mammograms were ordered. After some running around (my husband drove to another site and physically carried my former mammogram slides to the surgeon for a comparison), I waited. My breast was crushed by the machine and then I waited some more.

The slides eventually revealed some sort of mass of considerable size. A biopsy would be required. It was difficult to see the mass well through all the breast tissue. The whole debate about mammograms is ridiculous, in my opinion. Having them done did not help me to find cancer in the early stages, but they're a valuable diagnostic tool for those women who are saved by them! It's the same for throat cultures or any medical test. Perhaps you'll find strep through a culture and the next fellow won't.

I don't remember much about the time between the visit to the surgeon and my biopsy. In a trance, I got through being cheerful in front of the kids when they returned home from school. My husband and I were fitting appointments in while the children were in class. We didn't have family in the area so we managed by dashing about most weekday mornings.

The biopsy was arranged and I watched nervously as it was performed under local anesthesia. My breast was aching from the biopsy and the surgeon was explaining how he'd looked at the slides with the pathologist. The cells were arranged in lines, military fashion, and he was sure they were malignant. It was breast cancer. He wrote a prescription for a sedative (that I didn't fill) and asked to see us the following day when we'd had a chance to digest the news. Unless I could be shot with an elephant's tranquilizer dart, the sedative pills didn't seem worth doing. Besides, I had once read about drugs straining the liver and, I figured, I'd probably have a reaction. With my current luck, I'd have complications, right? In a masochistic fashion, I decided to stay alert.

During the 40 minute ride home, I cried my eyes out. I sobbed to my husband that I didn't want to die. I couldn't comprehend how my body had betrayed me and I just wanted to hack off my breasts. There was a lot of research to do and so much that I didn't understand. What did the surgeon mean: breast cancer? He told me that I had a large tumor and that there would be decisions to make. He added that the cancer was a lobular type. Were there different kinds of breast cancer? What was lobular?

On the radio, there was some sort of disco hour. I suddenly heard the BeeGees' "Staying Alive." I cried harder. Funny how songs can take on new meanings. I couldn't accept that I had been diagnosed with breast cancer. Just before our move, I had been painfully aware of the horrible time that a dear friend went through after finding a small lump. She had eventually died. She had three young children similar in age to our own. My kids had just turned 13, 10, and 7. How could I tell them? We decided on the truth: I'd found a lump; it was cancerous; but we weren't sure what would be done yet and that we'd keep them posted. My kids noticed that I didn't look "sick." How do you explain that, with cancer, the treatment is sometimes worse than the disease? I did feel fine physically, but it was draining to maintain the day-to-day routines and keep all our spirits up. When the kids went to school, then I worried and let myself release my emotions. Looking back, it probably would've been all right to have cried in front of the kids. Plenty of tears came later.

Chapter II

Scrambling For Answers

I stumbled around for days in a type of Twilight Zone. The world no longer made sense. I wanted my old life back. We met with the surgeon who'd performed the biopsy. He saw that I was a wreck and he tried to balance the news of a big tumor with some reassuring remarks. We didn't know if the lymph nodes were involved. There were different approaches available for dealing with tumors. The surgeon suggested that we could try to shrink it first, through chemotherapy, and then operate. His partner, who later removed the stitches from the biopsy, recommended a lumpectomy. "There's no difference statistically," he informed me.

Statistics. They were grim. My brain froze. I could no longer write or sing; both activities that I had previously enjoyed. Keeping food on the table and doing household chores somehow happened. I spent every spare moment cruising the Internet for information, scanning books, articles, an even talking to women who'd been through cancer treatments. I called a hotline in Chicago, the "Y-Me" organization, and became one of those desperate individuals who'd chat with strangers. I was used to being in control and self-reliant. Everywhere I turned, however, the situation seemed out of control.

"Options" were presented. There didn't seem to be conclusive data about breast cancer. Some of the information was contradicted by recent studies. Perusing the so-called latest material on the subject only confused me. How could it be that a lumpectomy was as effective as a mastectomy? What if you didn't "get it all?" As for shrinking the tumor, I wanted it the hell out of my body as soon as possible!

I couldn't find books that reflected real research on survivors. What had they done about their cancer? All the doctors kept emphasizing that it would be my decision. They talked about different choices. I had this warped idea that it was as if we were choosing between a roast beef sandwich or a tuna sub. In matter of fact tones, the menu was presented to me, but no one was saying, "...if you do this, you'll be better." I wanted to hear those words, but there were no guarantees coming with any option.

Through my reading, I learned why a lobular breast cancer was different from a ductal type. The lobular ones sounded "sneakier" to me. Fear set in more with each new book. I bought Susan Love's work which was supposed to be the "breast cancer bible." I purchased the Harvard Women's Health Handbook. I tried looking at inspirational stories and articles by health gurus who thought that "mind over matter" would help. I became overwhelmed by information. Some of the cancer material I'd requested from the National Cancer Society began coming in the mail. The treatment options looked medieval.

Many books harped on the extension of life. I was greedy: I wanted to beat cancer, not stall for time. In these books the patients were grateful for every extra day. After being shocked and frightened, I lost some of my numbness and got angry. Why weren't there more advances with this disease? I became a militant feminist. If men were threatened with losing private body parts which were dear to them, wouldn't there be a cure by now?

I read Simonton's, Getting Well Again. A major theme

involves recognizing and dealing with the forces which may have contributed to your disease. Had I put everyone else before myself? Was I a person who stewed over things and took them to heart? Had I been under stress? Could it be possible that I was somehow responsible for having breast cancer?!

Wallowing in self-analysis, I couldn't come up with any clear answers. What had caused my breast cancer? By concentrating on the cause, I lost the ability to focus on a possible cure. Like a character in a dramatic film, my life flashed before my eyes. I went over everything in the past: tensions, feelings of betrayal, and other emotions. Pollution seemed to be a strong explanation. We'd lived in Wilmington, Delaware for about 17 years; a state with one of the highest cancer rates. The chemical industry was located there. I used to joke that our water supply could develop film, based on the probability of finding chemicals in it. We, therefore, had a top-notch filter. It also dawned on me that my generation was the first to have food additives, "chem lawn," and other exposures. I remember that as kids, at the seashore, we used to chase the trucks which sprayed insecticide for mosquito control.

Breast cancer is called a lifestyle disease. I didn't fit the profile, though. I'd only gained about 10 pounds since having children. I thought that we led a good existence. Since most women face cancer or heart trouble when they're elderly, I figured that I'd be dealing with one or the other only when I was old. After extensive and exhausting research, I concluded that I needed more opinions. It didn't seem fair that I had the disease; it was also unjust that I was forced to interpret so much on my own.

My husband had a business contact who was plugged into the New York medical scene. She arranged for me to have an appointment with one of Manhattan's top surgeons. Once more, my husband physically drove all over to round up my biopsy report, my mammograms, and other information. Armed with these materials in a packet, we took the Amtrak to Penn Station.

My parents cannot be raved about enough. They flew into action and watched the kids, ran the household, and pitched in to make it possible for me to check out other doctors' advice. They later helped continually during my treatments. One warm April day, we came out of Penn Station. My husband and I reassured each other that we'd get answers. A famous surgeon was bound to know what to do and we thought that we were lucky to get to see him. We worried that, ever since the biopsy, the tumor had been tampered with and now time was of the essence. Our concern was subsequently "pooh-poohed;" the first of many notions which some doctors dismissed. I maintain that there's a lot they don't know.

Catching a cab, we also caught a typical scene: A guy was roller blading in the insane traffic while exposing himself. Since no one seemed to give him any attention, I laughed long and hard. Yes, it was good to be in New York. My world wasn't the only crazy place.

We met the surgeon and he had me instantly petrified. Lobular cancer can be tricky. He gravely explained that I had a large tumor and that it wasn't certain whether or not the cancer had already spread elsewhere. He could set up some tests. We decided to do a bone scan, chest x-ray, and some blood work to see where I stood. One lesson I learned immediately: It takes time to carry out medical procedures. We had to endure waiting, wondering, and being at the mercy of a huge bureaucracy. After what seemed to be endless pacing, I was injected with a dye and told to return in an hour for my first scan. We walked around Manhattan. When we later reconvened with the surgeon, he had some results in hand. The cancer did not appear to be in the bone yet. I almost collapsed in relief. What the surgeon proposed was a modified, radical mastectomy. He thought that the size of the tumor warranted that approach. I asked if he should remove both breasts; the right one as a preventative measure.

I must admit that "prevention" is not a well-known word in the cancer field. The doctor explained that he was only willing to operate on the left breast, but that he could biopsy the right breast to check for cancer there. I almost said that I was "dying to know if it were on the other breast," yet the word "dying" stuck in my throat. Words were even taking on new significance. On the train back to Pennsylvania, however, I wondered how a random biopsy could reveal enough. We were practically ready to schedule surgery with this fellow, but doubts and questions remained.

We'd heard that a guy at the University of Pennsylvania would be worth meeting. Ever since the diagnosis, we had tried to network with anyone who'd had an experience with cancer. It pays to talk to as many individuals as you can find. It was in this manner that we found the surgeon's name. Our home is located between Chadds Ford and Kennett Square so a trip to Philadelphia was under the hour. I liked the idea of being closer to our house and, one-stop shopping had arrived at the cancer industry there: A patient could see a surgeon and speak to an oncologist at the same center. Hmm. We decided to go.

The surgeon at the University of Pennsylvania had great people skills. He seemed to respect that I was loaded down with questions and didn't appear put out by them. I told him that I was worried. I wanted to be as aggressive as possible in my case. If I were eighty, maybe a wait and see approach would work. I was determined that, since the tumor was large, it would be best to be rid of both breasts. He understood. I don't know if I was more scared or relieved. The surgeon agreed to do a bilateral mastectomy. He also concurred with the fellow in New York that a mastectomy was the only good option. So much for the lumpectomy suggestion in Delaware. Surgery was set for May 8.

I recall throwing up when I became conscious again. The anesthesia can cause that reaction. I had a morphine drip hooked up to my arm. Bed rails kept me confined. My husband peered over me in concern. He had tried to see if he could retrieve some of my cells. Being a scientist himself, he thought that maybe a vaccine could be developed from my own cancer cells. Although the idea was applauded, the conditions in the operating room prevented the plan from being put into practice. At the time, I didn't know anything about what he'd attempted. He also didn't talk about how my cells were sent to the pathology department.

There were tubes on each side of my body with plastic containers hanging from them. They reminded me of turkey basters. I had a morbid curiosity to see my chest, but I was covered in bandages. An overworked nurse checked on me occasionally. The surgery had gone well. I was still groggy and unable to eat. Little did I realize that the nausea I had would be the first of many, many episodes. My wish to go home was granted within two days. Check ups back at the hospital were required, of course. Another nurse suggested that, while home, I keep a journal so that I could stay in touch with my feelings. I wanted to scream back, "Are you crazy? My feelings couldn't be any closer to the surface--I don't need to write about them, too!"

In my situation, there wasn't time to be upset about losing my breasts. All of my anxiety centered upon hearing the results of the pathology report. I hadn't had swollen lymph nodes so we were hoping that the cancer was contained to the tumor site. It started to become clear to us that the surgeon, although excellent, wouldn't be the key player. We had to find a trustworthy oncologist. Now that the tumor was gone, what should we do? It seemed obvious that there would be chemotherapy, however, we required more information.

I was given painkillers. I only took a minimal amount of them because the physical pain was trivial compared to the mental strain. The waiting was awful. Pathology reports take time. After about five days, we bugged the surgeon's office. They promised to get back to us. The first call my husband received was good news. Unfortunately, he was called back moments later with other results. My surgeon was a compassionate guy and the pathology report had surprised him. It turned out that I had aggressive cells; spots of cancer on the right breast; and the cancer had spread to 31 lymph nodes. I figured that it was all over.

I was already berserk over the fact that we were the

ones making all of the decisions. We weren't medical doctors. Pure instinct had taken over when I'd opted for a bilateral mastectomy. I kept thinking: What if I'd listened to the doctor who'd urged me to have a lumpectomy? Analyzing what had happened didn't matter. I had to know if it could be medically possible to overcome my condition.

There was some debate whether I had Stage IV or end of Stage III cancer. There are only four stages. It depended upon whether one viewed the cancer spots on the right breast as having formed simultaneously with the tumor or whether they were a sign of metastasis or "spread." We spoke with an oncologist at the University of Pennsylvania. He answered my question by blurting out, "It's a crapshoot." I tried to absorb the fact: Whether or not I lived was a crapshoot.

I told the oncologist that I believed oncology was the same as meteorology in that case. If the weatherman predicts sun and it rains instead, he isn't to blame. Neither field appeared to have any accountability. I used to have a running joke with my husband called, "What's wrong with this picture?" Sometimes, absurd situations arose and the line was appropriate. I shook my head in disbelief that this learned man truly couldn't tell me anything.

I tried to concentrate on the oncologist's recommendations, but he didn't sound optimistic about them. He mentioned a bone marrow transplant, after chemotherapy; followed by radiation; and taking tamoxifen indefinitely. There was a new protocol, he explained, which consisted of: four months of high dose chemotherapy; go into the bone marrow treatment; and do the rest all within about a half year's time.

Bone marrow transplant? I couldn't believe that what I was hearing pertained to me. My cynical side took over. Was this doctor needing someone for a research study? I was already reeling from learning about clinical studies in which you could end up with a placebo. Hey, I wasn't a child of the sixties for nothing. It seemed time for another opinion.

We'd only been in our new school district for a few months, but I'd managed to meet a wonderful teacher who'd been through her own hell. During a volunteer stint in her classroom, she'd let me know that she'd had ovarian cancer. As part of her treatment, both her breasts were removed. Since she'd lived in the area a long time, I decided to call her for a suggestion about a local oncologist. Besides being bothered by the "newness" of the proposal, logistical problems were dawning on me. My husband had been a doll, but I didn't want him having to commute unnecessarily. I also wasn't sure that I wanted chemotherapy in an enormous institution. The teacher recommended her oncologist and said that he was trained at the University of Pennsylvania. He was located about 20 minutes away in West Chester and we arranged to see him.

I was having trouble believing that I could survive. The oncologist didn't offer false hope, but he said that it wasn't over either. There were techniques that could be tried. He was sincere, caring, and best of all for me, had a sense of humor. Although comedic talents aren't the top priority for an oncologist, his demeanor was what I needed. He was intelligent, up to date on the latest treatment options, but more importantly, he thought that I could get well. He also explained that trying the four months of chemo was still technically doing something experimental. He stuck with the traditional six months of treatment. The bone marrow transplant was an experimental procedure so why do one experiment on top of another? Although there wasn't solid proof that the bone marrow treatment worked, he thought that I should include it. My treatments would then take about a year, with radiation coming last. He also said that high doses of chemo would now be possible due to the advent of a drug that could be injected for several days each month.

Was high dose chemo more effective than a regular dose? No one knew for sure, but it was supposed that if a little bit could kill cancer then having a lot might nuke the cells. Being in the oncologist's office was an "out of body" experience. I glanced around the waiting room. Most of the patients were elderly and I resented being among them. I was glad, though, that we'd found an oncologist and that I could start trying to destroy the cancer. My chemotherapy began three weeks after my surgery.

Chapter III
Chemo Brain

I was fortunate to find my oncologist. The office staff was pleasant and the surroundings were more like my dentist's than a place of disease. My orientation included meeting the nurses who tapped into my veins, getting information about the drugs (CAF), and a description of a typical chemo cycle. I was due to have some heavy-duty compounds and an obscene sounding one called 5 f-u. If you've ever looked up the side effects on a cough medicine label, you can imagine how flipped out I was when I read about these babies. Every office visit included a blood test to see the blood profile, especially the white cell counts, before I was given another set of toxins.

In order to show up for my chemotherapy, I had to shop around for a padded bra or prosthesis. The tubes on my sides had been literally yanked out. I tried to consider the advantages of being breastless. I could play the guitar without having any boobs get in the way. I alternated between hope and despair each day. I wouldn't be described as a laid-back person. When cancer hit, it was hard to calm down. I tried using some meditation and visualization techniques that I'd read about, but I wasn't a quick learner. (More on that later.) Meanwhile, I decided that I didn't want the kids stumbling across Mommy's fake breasts and I opted for a padded bra. I'd located a store in Delaware which supposedly sold a specially fitted bra that could hold "falsies."

My mother accompanied me on this outing. She used the excuse of driving me because my arms and chest were still sore, but she was insistent on coming with me for moral support. I told the salesgirl that I'd had surgery due to breast cancer and that I was looking for "falsies." She was a young thing with a huge cleavage and she gave me a blank look. I attempted to explain again what I needed. The salesgirl expressed sympathy for my plight and acted as if I had a headcold. "Well, maybe you'll be over it soon. I knew a lady who had breast cancer and she's fine. They found a little spot on her mammogram." By now I was ready to strangle her. "...a little spot." Why couldn't I have required the smallest amount of surgery or just tamoxifen? Why didn't this bimbo know what "falsies" are?

My mom marveled at her ignorance. After a few more minutes of clarification, the salesgirl beamed at us. "Oh, oh, I see, you mean 'deceivers.' Yes, I have a bra which you can fit deceivers into."

It turned out that deceivers are exactly the same as falsies, of course. I started to giggle. It was ridiculous. I understood that hoagies in the Philadelphia area can be called subs elsewhere, but now I wondered what regions referred to falsies as "deceivers."

Equipped with my new deceivers, my husband brought me to my first chemotherapy session while my parents waited anxiously at our home. I was getting to be a pro in regard to anti-nausea drugs after the hospital stay. As the first liquid filled the tube, which was suspended from the ceiling on a plant hook, I was surprised to see its pink color. I asked instead about the pills that would supposedly prevent vomiting.

The room where the chemo was administered was loaded with armchairs, afghans, and cozy pillows. The chairs' occupants were engaged in various activities. To my horror, one old lady was wolfing down potato chips while the medicine dripped into her. A man with bushy eyebrows gave me a "it's your first time isn't it" type wink. Considering that we were all having some form of poison, the den type room achieved a cheerful decor. It was at the oncologist's office of the University of Pennsylvania where the patients looked like holocaust victims. I had dubbed it the "Land of the Living Dead," because of the look in patients' eyes. To my immense relief, my chemotherapy room didn't remind me of concentration camp scenes.

Returning home, I was a bit dazed. The nausea didn't set in right away. It was on the day after chemo that I was violently ill. The drugs did prevent some vomiting and mostly, I was just tired. The space cadet feeling and lack of energy were due as much to being drained emotionally as to the chemo itself. I was supposed to return for another dose the next week. My blood counts had dropped dramatically, but I was able to still have the chemotherapy. I came back to the office for weekly blood tests and to have syringes drawn up so that I could inject myself with a drug which spurs white cell growth. Nursing would not be my chosen profession. Some patients let the real nurses administer their shots; I decided to "swab and stab" at home, based upon an instructional video that the office provided.

My emotions were all over the place. It was now June and, fortunately, not flu season. I had to watch out for infection with such low blood counts. My oncologist wanted me to eventually do a liver scan for a baseline image--something to compare my liver with when the chemo was finished. More decisions were needed. What was I going to do about my mental state? How about nutrition? My hair would start falling out and was I going to wear hats or a wig?

My dive into the medical ocean began. I drank barium in order to have a CAT scan of my liver. I decided to be neurotic about germs and to try keeping my chemo on schedule. No more movies in theaters or shopping in large stores. When it was time for my second cycle of chemo, my oncologist was away and his partner shaved back my dose. I was disappointed because I wanted the cancer attacked. My blood counts were low and later there would be slight delays in having chemo while waiting for my body to recover from the various hits. I was also getting anemic. I started having intense vaginal bleeding. As usual, I just figured that I was falling apart.

I met a cancer survivor who proved to be a friend and valuable resource. She told me that chemo had pushed her into menopause. Why was I bleeding then? She also put me in touch with a woman who visited my home and showed me her selection of wigs. I ordered a simple, short look and, when it was delivered, shoved it in the back of my closet. My uncle teased me that it was my chance to be a blond, but I stuck with something close to my old appearance. I ordered a few turbans to wear around the house because summer humidity could make wig-wearing a hassle.

My bleeding eventually slowed down and then stopped. My hair was another story. It fell out in huge clumps. I'd awaken in the morning, not remembering my current situation for a moment, and then realize that my curls were all over the pillow. Some patients cut their hair very short so they don't see as much hair going. I couldn't do anything. Somehow, a numbness or "automatic pilot" set in and I watched as my hair dropped off in clumps. My scalp also tingled with pain.

The liver scan had revealed what we hoped were benign

cysts. A scan at the end of my chemo would show if there were any changes. If the cysts got bigger or smaller, it could be cancer. Meanwhile, I was still boning up on the whole cancer industry. It seemed that some doctors didn't even check your liver; each institution had slightly different approaches to chemo; and some fields of research were just dormant.

We had stumbled across some information about progesterone and the role of hormones in breast cancer. When my cells were analyzed, there were contradictory results: After the biopsy, the cells were labeled "slightly estrogen positive," but following the mastectomies, there was a "no estrogen response" report. I had hoped that a high "estrogen response" would have meant the likelihood of tamoxifen or of an estrogen blocker being effective. It kept looking as if all of my data fell into the worst categories.

I had clung to the news that there were "clean margins" after surgery. Essentially, it meant that the doctor didn't find traces of more cancer in the tissue surrounding the tumor. We were starting to require a glossary to comprehend all the medical terms and their implications.

One of my chemo hits occurred on Halloween. It seemed appropriate. I joked with my kids that I could scare off the neighbors if I took off the wig. I teased my husband that I was developing multiple personalities. One minute I could absorb myself in the family routine, but the next I'd be alone and crying. The pendulum kept swinging between gratitude that I was with my family and fear over whether I would stay with them.

I couldn't concentrate on much of anything. I've been informed by other cancer veterans that it's called "chemo brain." Some days I was almost in a trance. In waiting rooms, I didn't read any magazines; I simply sat in a semi-catatonic state. I was slow to react and was often drained. There are many new anti-nausea drugs which have prevented symptoms in patients. A woman I knew wasn't even queasy once. Unfortunately, I could count on a few days each month when my head was in a bucket.

The cancer statistics were my biggest nightmare. I would also glance at my chart and see that I was labeled in the advanced breast cancer category. According to many of my books, I had only a 10-15% chance of being around in five years. The size of my tumor and the huge number of lymph nodes that showed cancer in them, put me in a high risk category for a recurrence. I sobbed during one of my chemo sessions. The nurses kindly gave me a pep talk and emphasized that my "category" was defined for treatment decision purposes. It had nothing to do with my outcome, they explained. One nurse added that once you have over 10 positive lymph nodes, it didn't matter that I had 31. With a lot of compassion, the staff hinted that maybe I was at the stage where I should consider that "ignorance is bliss." I had read myself into a saturation point of information and the more statistical analyses I saw, the more depressed I became.

They were right. I stopped reading because my decisions were all made except one: I had to learn more about the bone marrow transplant and decide if I was going to do it. For the chemotherapy, it was time to accept it and hope it was effective. Just prior to my information strike, I had searched the internet. When there are over a couple hundred thousand entries on a topic, one wonders how to sift through the material. I had found one guy who compared his chemotherapy to having an orgasm. More power to him if he thought that he'd discovered a way to enjoy it! A woman who saw breast cancer as a male, corporate plot, had decided against surgery and chemotherapy. She was using alternative therapies and she believed that her breast cancer was caused from her deodorant. Women shave their underarms and, through years of having heavy metals from deodorants seep into their bloodstreams, then lumps form with high frequency near their armpits.

I logged off the computer. It was time for me to concentrate on withstanding the chemotherapy and not becoming ill. I bought diaper wipes and carried them around with me. If I shopped for groceries, I wiped the cart handle down first. I found anti-bacterial soap for the family to use. A friend going through divorce gave me an "affirmation" speech. She was in a group which told themselves how wonderful and strong they were each day. She said that I must insist that I have a tough mind and body.

Laughter was perhaps the best medicine. I no longer watched any movie, television show, or news item of a depressing nature. The only images on the screen were comedies. In our area, Seinfeld re-runs were aired at 7:30

pm. The whole family would gather to watch Jerry and his buddies. I felt guilty that we didn't read with the children then; we snuggled up and laughed, though. My father prepared video tapes of funny programs. We enjoyed Tim Stack in a hilarious send-up of talk shows called, "Nightstand." It was one of those programs shown at midnight, but was later available on the "E" (Entertainment) Network. The chuckles were a form of therapy.

My attempts at visualization and meditation, two recommended techniques for cancer patients, weren't going well. The concept behind visualization is that you might create a synergistic effect with the chemo if you could picture your cancer cells being destroyed. Patients have imagined battleships or lasers wiping out their cancer. The verdict's out whether your mind helps the medicine. I think that for some individuals, it works. It was a useful exercise for me because I felt as if I were actively helping. It also gave me something to keep working at while I was driving myself nuts with worry.

I began with Viking ships, but then I went high tech. When the chemo was administered, I closed my eyes and concentrated upon different forces attacking the cancer. It was good to imagine the bad cells being conquered.

Meditation was a problem. When I took natural childbirth classes, we thought that my husband should have had the babies. He was able to relax and meditate himself into a deep state of rest. I was always restless. I'm still not able to transport myself to another realm, but I've gotten the knack of slowing my system down. I believe that it's very important to relax your body. The sheer anxiety of the time cannot be of benefit to the immune system which is already struggling with the disease.

Looking back, I was never hyper yet I often ran on adrenaline. It probably wasn't healthy to be pumped up over issues and events. A calm demeanor is less taxing on the body. I've developed a completely non-medical theory about our immune systems: I think that we erode our systems through various means and often without recognizing what we've done. The immune system was the key to overcoming cancer. Could I kill off enough cancer cells so that my immune system could function well? By having cancer, I had impaired the very mechanism that should be dealing with abnormal cells. We all might have some cancer in us but healthy immune systems deal with the cells. Something had caused my system to break down. When my chemotherapy was finished, we still wouldn't have any means of measuring if it "worked." Only time will tell was an awful way of saying that if you're alive, then maybe the harmful cells were scaled back enough for the body to deal with them.

Fear of germs had resulted in somewhat of a withdrawal from the world. In my case, the precautions were worth it because I had more treatments after chemo. I appeared to be in menopause, which brought a new host of symptoms. My thermostat seemed broken. I was either freezing or having hot flashes. My left arm became stiff, but I hadn't joined any "post mastectomy" exercise group. Exercise, however, I did. Every day, rain or shine, I walked around my neighborhood. Besides being beneficial to my chemo brain, the oxygen was important. I stayed in shape and actually built up my stamina while my white cells plummeted. Sometimes I had some shortness of breath, but I kept on walking. I believe that through walking, I also convinced myself that I was alive. "Hey, I'm still walking around," had become my answer to well-meaning people who inquired about me.

Besides counting on vomiting each month, my voice began to get raspy and low. At one of my checkups, I told my oncologist that I couldn't sing or play the guitar anymore. I found out that he was a guitarist, too. He made me a deal: When the treatments are over, we'll have a guitar jam. My eyes teared up because although he couldn't promise I'd be around, I concluded that he would not have proposed a music session if he didn't believe that there was a possibility for survival.

My senses became sharpened, also. I called it the "Stop and Smell the Roses Syndrome." I was constantly commenting to my amused family, "Oh, look at the cardinal, isn't it gorgeous? Did you see the robin get the worm? The forsythia came out so yellow, don't you think?"

My kids gradually just shrugged, "Mom is into this nature thing again."

The fog on my chemo brain was lifting. I still had trouble paying attention to details, but I was more aware of the world around me. For such a long time, the horrible shock of the diagnosis and the rush into treatment hadn't left room for other contemplations. I started to notice things again.

Chapter IV

Family, Friends, and Support

I'm indebted to my family. They were my support group. My husband, my children, my parents, and even extended family kept me going. My husband's family is in Europe; they stayed constantly in touch. My cousins, aunts, and uncles, checked in on me and called regularly. I often thought how difficult it must be for cancer patients without close-knit families. I would hope that, in such a situation, friends could serve the function of boosting spirits and lending a hand.

My parents are wise, loving, generous people. I'm the oldest of four girls; I was born in Philadelphia. My father taught at Germantown High and was an administrator at Edison High. My mother has a degree in elementary education. We lived a modest existence in Pennsylvania until I was a teen. My father began a corporate job in Manhattan. High school was completed in New Jersey; my folks subsequently moved to Stamford, Connecticut when the company relocated there.

My father worked hard and improved our position through the years. Due to my parents, I was able to attend Boston University's School of Public Communication. I met my husband in Cambridge, Massachusetts. My parents are progressive, informed, individuals, who didn't even blink when I brought home an Icelander as my fiancee. I'd always been interested in other cultures. I'd gone abroad as an American Field Service (AFS) exchange student to France, after high school. In college, I'd minored in Spanish and attended the Universidad de los Andes, in Bogota, Colombia, as an exchange student. Eventually, I completed a master's degree in cross-cultural communication.

I've always been proud of my family's open-mindedness. We weren't raised with any formal religious affiliation, but we were taught to respect everyone. I have relatives in love with people of different religions and races. My whole family is like a mini United Nations. Compared to other American households, we were a bit unconventional. Instead of attending a church or synagogue, my family spent a lot of time in volunteer service. We learned that it was vital to give back to the community. My mother used to run, and is still active with, the "Meals on Wheels" program and she is involved in a number of other non-profit groups. My father served on library boards; gave free consulting services to the Salvation Army; and still volunteers for several organizations.

When I was diagnosed with breast cancer, many other patients told me how much their faith mattered to them. I didn't have a religious institution to turn to and I was reluctant to start with something because of my illness. Longwood Gardens, containing a gorgeous collection of plant species from around the world, is located nearby. As a pass holder to the gardens, I took solitary rambles there and "communed with nature." I suppose that it was my form of prayer. I was lucky to have a beautiful setting down the road, so I spent long hours contemplating my fate amidst the shrubs and flowers.

A friend from South America called me and wanted to arrange for me to see a "healer." I'd also met people with cancer who worshipped daily. Some saw their existence to be in God's hands and they were surprisingly calm. I envied their tranquillity. I don't put any method down that a cancer patient can use to relax. Prayer is an effective means of soothing the soul. It's crucial to find any comfort you can while dealing with cancer.

I had considered seeing a psychologist because I sometimes awoke at night with panic attacks. Since I didn't have a personal relationship with anyone, it struck me as the same as suddenly seeking out religion. The only psychologist I knew socially was inclined to speak of preparing for death, upon hearing that I had an advanced case of cancer. I chose not to be on the couch. I have heard, however, of patients who have been tremendously helped by therapists. Again, your own instincts will determine what's right for you.

It had come to my attention that a new field was gaining credibility called, "healing touch." There were cardiac patients who'd come through surgery with the aid of healing touch techniques. Cancer patients had found a relaxing sense of "wellness" after being worked on by a trained healer. I was offered the chance to try it. Originally skeptical, I became convinced that it was more effective with me than meditation. I was forced to concentrate my mind on calming down my system. Some of the practices sound far out. The healer "opens" your body through hand motions. In a certain respect, healing touch is based on magnetic fields and an attempt to balance them. Before I had cancer, I would have looked askance at the whole thing, but now I endorse anything that keeps your immune system calm.

One of my cousins is into "new age" stuff and she believes in healing music with incense as a means to relax. I was moved by how many relatives kept coming up with suggestions for me. I know some patients go for "aromatherapy," but I never tried it. I do draw the line at obvious scams, but if the procedure isn't harmful I can't knock it. I think that the important point is that you believe that something is working. I'm not so sure that it matters what we do in addition to our treatments, as long as we convince ourselves that it will help.

The mind's role in cancer is perplexing. On the one hand, I don't want the guilt that I can somehow control what my body's doing. The flip side that I'm capable of healing myself, however, is appealing. I wish that every cancer survivor could be interviewed to find out what was done to last. It may never be possible to establish a scientific relationship between one's mental powers and physical health, but my gut feeling is that some type of relationship does exist.

Both my mother and father had a brother who smoked like a chimney. My Mom's brother had recently passed away from lymphoma. My Dad's brother had been diagnosed with inoperable lung cancer when I started my chemotherapy. My Uncle had lost his wife to breast cancer and he'd written a thesis on the topic of cancer. Many years later, he was fortunate to marry again, and they lived on the same street in Philadelphia as my cousin, his daughter, and her family. My uncle was in his mid-sixties and, except for chemo, there wasn't much that could be done. Before he died, we had several conversations about cancer because we'd always been close. My uncle, a pragmatist, thought that I should discuss my wishes with my husband and make plans for the children. My husband was in denial about anything happening to me and he refused to even mention the subject.

I don't know what's best for families. My parents, although extremely worried, managed to convey to me that they thought I might be one of the few people who pull through. All that I do know is, it was vital to me to realize that there were individuals who did not regard me as dying. Hope is a word with new meanings for me. The most hardened realist cannot afford to lose hope.

I could never say enough about my husband. He was my rock. We'd always been close but he was amazing. He worked so hard to research my situation and he tackled my cancer as if it were his full time job to learn about it. My children were so concerned, but we maintained a fairly normal existence for them. Other than cutting back activities and watching out for infection, they continued with school and depended upon my parents. When they'd return home from school, they'd check on me. They probably wanted the reassurance that I was in the bedroom. They handled the worry differently. They all became a little withdrawn from friends while keeping their own routines. We only answered the questions they raised and didn't tell them more than they wanted to know.

Friends were shocked when they heard about me. At first, there was an outpouring of flowers, cards, inspirational books, etc. My friends quickly fell into one of three types: We know that you'll get through this ordeal encouragers;

oh, if it's an advanced case, hmm, we're uncomfortable around you; and morbid curiosity newsgathering callers. I'll always remember the people who stuck by me through all of the treatments. I was also touched by acquaintances who'd sent me "thinking of you" messages and offers of help. I had too many memories of making dinners for my friend, before she died, so I turned down the kind intentions. I had nightmares about when she was in hospice. I can still see the oxygen tanks which were in the front hallway when I dropped off meals.

Later, when in the hospital, I allowed some friends to bring dinners to my parents while they ran the household. I was proud that I had only asked one woman, one time, to watch my son for an hour when I had a blood test scheduled. My parents took over the childcare and we were very independent. It was a foolish attitude of mine, but I had trouble accepting assistance.

I had wonderful offers. My friend in Chicago was ready to jump on a plane and help me. Relatives and friends wanted to be with the kids. Some friends never realized that by treating me as they always had, they were giving me the best gift: moral support. There's nothing worse than losing your pride and your identity. I'd already lost my breasts and my hair. I was able to function a bit and needed to do so. You may have cancer, but you're the same person afterall. Being a charity case or a hopeless case won't contribute to a recovery. Even if the cancer experience changes you, your friends should see you as a person and not only as a patient.

I'm from the generation which recognized "bad vibes." I tried to avoid people who didn't make me feel "up." I didn't want to hurt anyone's feelings, but I couldn't deal with people who didn't have a positive outlook. The friends who managed to communicate that they believed, "...this too shall pass," were the ones I allowed into my life.

Bernie Siegel and other cancer author gurus urge us to act out of forgiveness and love. Negative emotions, such as anger and bitterness, will not add to your healing process. I was still dwelling on some issues that had arisen prior to our move. To understand, I'll provide this brief background: It wasn't surprising that I'd be interested in social causes, given my family's attitudes. My husband and I had moved to Delaware when forced busing began. We wanted our children to have the diversity of the schools there. Through the years, I became active on the school scene. I served on several district committees and ran a district-wide organization while still volunteering in the schools. Running after three kids, I was a free-lance writer and cross-cultural communications consultant. It was ideal because I worked from home and only accepted occasional assignments.

Delaware is such a small state; it's inevitable that if you're involved with educational issues, then you become sucked into politics. All I had ever wanted to do was make things better there. It was horrible to see young children who couldn't read in third grade. We fought for small class sizes; better funding; and other causes. Depending upon who was on the school board, decisions affecting the children were bouncing around while discipline and other problems mounted. A new superintendent, with animosity toward the community, ran through dollars and he discontinued good programs. I became indignant on behalf of friends and personnel who were mistreated at the time. I was an expert at vicarious indignation.

Our eldest daughter had been bused into the city as part of the desegregation plan. By fifth grade, she found needles on the playground at recess; saw her teacher robbed; and witnessed a child beating. Her curriculum was great, but the school was run-down and lacking basic supplies. Our two other children began their school with: a child molester just released nearby; an arsonist having burnt down part of the school; and the defeat of a tax referendum which would have offered some relief to the district.

After many years of understanding that being involved meant treatment as a heroine or a villain, it had seemed worth the effort because we'd brought about some decent changes. We now thought that the school situation appeared futile. We knew that we had to find new schools for the kids. It was an intense, bitter time in the school district as dissatisfaction with the superintendent and money woes resulted in personal attacks on parents trying to improve the system. We had wanted to remain in our home which we had enjoyed tremendously. Private school tuition costs were too high, however, so we decided to move.

When our son was put in a classroom with a teacher who was a substitute with no prior experience, we were concerned. We then learned that the teacher would not have basic supplies until November. Second grade was too critical and we realized that we couldn't afford to wait for the house to sell before moving. It was a disappointment to bail out and it was a great expense. A new principal had also created an unpleasant atmosphere in the school and the strain was showing on our child. During the deterioration process of the schools, there was a sense of betrayal for those of us who'd dedicated huge chunks of our time to the system.

In retrospect, I was probably suffering from a mild sort of depression over conditions which I was powerless to affect. Nothing is hopeless. You can always do something about circumstances. You may have to swallow your pride or compromise, but you should never regard anything as futile. If your body is fighting disease then you should do your best to be rid of emotional baggage.

Analyzing and dealing with different relationships taught me to shed some mental weight. I needed all of my strength and energy to deal with the cancer. There was no room for soap operas nor draining experiences of any kind. One often hears about a "fighting attitude" that's important in cancer cases. I disagree. I think that the "fighting," if it only means not giving up, is alright. Staying pumped up and fighting is harmful. It's not good to take anything to heart, especially if it eats you up inside. A calm, steady, positive hope was more beneficial to me than a combative attitude. Sometimes I pictured myself being rid of past, negative emotions about people if I shook my hands in the air. Your anxiety of coping with the disease can drain you. Keep only your real friends around you and cancer has a way of determining who they are for you.

I had intended to join a support group. When I called to find out about one that met near me, I learned that the group had a new leader. The woman who'd run the breast cancer support for several years had been hospitalized with a recurrence. Completely spooked by the news, I used the excuse about germs and the importance of taking precautions as the reason not to attend meetings. The group met at an area hospital. I learned of another group in Delaware that was a spiritual, wellness clan. It was a generic support group, I suppose, that forbid wallowing in despair. No one was allowed to exchange horror stories. An acquaintance gave me the leader's phone number and I called to see if I'd be welcome.

"What is your sign?" she asked.

With a sinking feeling, I realized that a support group

believing in horoscopes might not be my thing. "Could you tell me about your group?" I responded instead.

"Our next meeting will be (she named a state park) and we're all going out to hug as many trees as we can!"

By now I was sure this was not the group for me. It turned out that the leader believed in life's force emanating from the ground and flowing from trees into us. She saw her own breast cancer going back into the earth and new life coming to her from the treetrunks. I never inquired if one species has more power over another. When I told the oncology nurse about it, she wondered which trees the group planned to hug. We had a good laugh; I complained that insects seemed attracted to my wig so maybe that was a sign; and then I never thought about support groups again.

What was scary to me, however, was that I couldn't truly put down the tree loving support group. The "we're in your face, cancer" psychology had an appeal. I can't be judgmental. I remembered television news features where some poor cancer patient was the victim of a treatment scam. What kind of individual takes advantage of a fellow human's desperation? We'd all draw the line over unscrupulous practices, but harmless methods of support don't bother me.

My family and friends were of such support that I was indeed fortunate. I've heard of patients who depended on their support groups comprising other cancer sufferers. There is certainly an experience gap when it comes to discussing "chemo brain." When my chemotherapy was finished, I did meet other women who were continuing to get together for understanding. In an informal manner, I've stayed in touch with some of them. We're a strange sorority. There is a connection among women with breast cancer. I admire those who've committed time to helping others through hotlines and organizations of support. Women are also recognizing that everyone requires different sorts of support. I kept counting my blessings. I still shudder to think of women without insurance to cover treatments. It might be one reason why the statistics are so awful.

Some important support also arrived from my husband's colleagues. An Icelandic guy, doing his residency at Yale's bone marrow unit, called to offer encouragement. He dismissed the frightening statistics by saying that they were cumulative and, therefore, did not reflect some of the recent progress. I didn't buy everything that he said, but he did give me a new outlook on the bone marrow transplant. The procedure had only been done in the last five or six years for breast cancer patients and the numbers did not yet show what happened to these women over time.

Now a word on our dog. We have a Shetland Sheepdog who is like my fourth child. When I was devastated by my cancer diagnosis, our dog refused to leave my side. Sensing my moods, he stayed with me everywhere I went in the house to the point that I was half tripping over him. It was something out of a Disney film. Our dog surpassed Lassie for caring. He still keeps near me and cocks his head to check on how I'm doing. I remember sometimes feeling ready to throw up and just petting him for comfort. The unconditional love of animals is powerful medicine, too.

Chapter V

Herb Tea and Nutrition

There's an old folk song that begins, "Who would've thunk it?" That line summarizes the dietary approach that I took. Other than special multi-vitamins during pregnancy and breast-feeding, I didn't pop much more than an occasional vitamin C. We had a balanced diet; not too much meat, but a little bit of every food group. What I consume now is different. "You are what you eat" makes sense.

Before I started my chemotherapy, I spoke with a nutritionist who'd been recommended by a friend. The nutritionist came to my home for a consultation. She raved about bioflavanoids and antioxidants and lost me entirely. The oncologists had figured that either you get the cancer or you don't; nutrition wasn't exactly a major aspect of their training. I didn't have the impression that they had much regard for it either, except for maintaining weight during chemotherapy. The nutritionist naturally thought that the chemo. didn't matter as much as the diet. She said that it would be hard to know what would appeal to me since the drugs would affect my taste buds, but she made some suggestions. I thought that I'd check out her ideas.

It was soon exasperating. Looking into what was supposedly best for you to eat was like taking a philosophy class. Before it was possible to determine whether or not a food helped, a belief accompanied the item. Some studies indicated that women in China and Japan had less breast cancer due to soy in their diets. Soy beans have fat, however, and I'd also learned that low-fat foods might be beneficial for me. We eventually compromised and bought some soy protein powder. Ginseng, which some cancer patients think enhances their immune systems, was cited in a Canadian study as something for breast cancer patients to avoid. Another study proposed having a diet based on wild yams because of the natural progesterone in them. Where in the world was I supposed to get wild yams and how many wild yam recipes exist?

A nutrition newsletter included a feature article about the importance of staying away from milk and dairy products. For breast cancer patients, the fat content from milk and cheeses would be harmful. Only low-fat cheese such as parmesan and mozzarella were worth having. Vitamins were even loonier. Antioxidant vitamins sounded great, but then I saw a study which said not to take them during radiation because they could interfere with the treatment. Hmm. So, take the vitamins during some treatments and not others. How much should one have? The vitamin bottle labels seemed to suggest huge amounts. Why wasn't there a system based on weight? Should I use the same quantity of vitamins as a 300 pound male?

Supplements were starting to be hawked everywhere. Who had heard of echinacea a few years ago? The women who were breast cancer survivors chose a wide range of approaches. One sipped her diet coke, ate cookies, went to McDonald's, and clogged her veins with hydrogenated oils and butter. Another lady kept to a strictly macrobiotic diet. She spent a large portion of her day in food shopping and preparation.

I initially tried for a middle of the road, rice and beans, cuisine. I was soon bored. For awhile, I mixed Ovaltine in skim milk and increased my fruits, vegetables, and grains.

One of my daughters decided to be a vegetarian (except during the summer when hamburgers on the grill were delicious) and I tried some tofu recipes with her. I cut out all caffeine (no chocolate, no coffee); reduced my sugar and salt intake; didn't eat any beef; and sampled salmon often (to get more cell-building Omega 3's).

An Icelandic woman suggested that I go on cod liver oil. By now, I also had garlic coming out of my pores, onion breath, and I was using all the home remedies since the cavemen's time so I gave cod liver oil a whirl, too. I liked the imagery about cod liver oil: It was supposed to have nutritional value, but keep my insides so slippery that the cancer couldn't spread. Well, I could grease up my digestive track. The trick was to find unpolluted cod liver oil and we bought only the arctic countries' products.

Exploring the supermarket with new dietary requirements, I came back disgusted. "If there's no fat, then there's a ton of sugar," I complained to my husband. "If there's no or low sugar, then there's a lot of sodium--come to think of it, there's sodium in practically everything!" I was now conscious of maintaining a sodium/potassium balance. In alarm over the American sodium diet, I added bananas (for potassium) to the daily regimen. Should I use organic foods? Once more, I was generating more questions than answers on a topic.

Ironically, my husband's corporation was preparing to launch a nutritional drink. It had been in clinical trials for arthritis sufferers and it had anti-inflammatory characteristics. It also had a protective effect on the gastrointestinal tract, which is often damaged with chemotherapy agents. I volunteered to be a guinea pig. I took the drink each day along with an ever expanding amount of supplements. My vitamins were at pretty much normal levels, but as I heard of a new herbal remedy, I investigated it. Aloe had healing properties. The liquid aloe was awful so I tried taking the aloe gel tablet. My attitude became: If it can't harm you, why not try it? Of course, given the thousands of herbal alternatives, this wasn't such a great outlook. I required a plan.

It was back to the books, only this time my husband did the research. He came across authors who swore they'd developed cancer cures through foods and vitamins. Doctors such as Kenneth Block, in Chicago, were treating advanced cancer patients with totally different diets and people were having their cancers disappear. This was astounding stuff and, as with treatment options, there weren't just various schools of thought--there were entire universities of opinion. What was right? Who did one believe? Studies kept contradicting certain practices.

We were suddenly aware of the medical revolution. When did Dr. Andrew Weil become noted as a genius and not dismissed as a nutcase? What was the Lexington and Concord of this movement? It seemed as if mainstream medicine was under siege. If sales of alternative medicinal products were any indication, the public no longer depended on conventional medicine alone. The testimonial approach was powerful: People were declaring that they'd rid themselves of various ailments and diseases with common herbs or plants.

Out of curiosity and partially to be sure that we'd unturned every stone, we located an alternative medicine practice. The guy running the organization had a satellite office near us. In a shabby room, not far from where the mushroom workers in Kennett Square had their headquarters, another medical world operated. There were shiny posters of acupuncture and shelves with multi-colored liquids in vials. The man behind the group had fought diabetes and controlled it through alternative medicine. The main doctor was his wife. She hailed originally from mainland China and had been a personal physician to an Egyptian leader before coming west.

They both seemed sincere about what they were doing and we decided to arrange for a consultation. They were a fascinating couple. He was a traveler to Tibet and would probably be great friends with Richard Gere. She was down to business at once and she demanded to see my tongue while taking my pulse.

After some questioning about my condition, they both told me that I must face death and say no to it. They could help me with herbs that had immune system boosting properties. They were currently working with other breast cancer patients and advising them about castor oil poultices along with supplements. To protect my liver, I was told to take milk thistle. They gave me some Chinese herbs that were blended in Holland. Red clover was suggested, too. They weren't enthusiastic about the bone marrow transplant because it brings the immune system down to nothing. Their medicine was based on keeping the body in harmony;

the immune system had to stay intact to fight disease. Part of me couldn't believe that I was soliciting their views. I was intrigued by their work, but I couldn't get over that I was resorting to such measures. The fact was that I was desperate to try anything.

My husband spent a few weeks deliberating over what was worth trying and what was not. Together we outlined a diet plan based on our own judgment and input we'd gathered. I teased him that either I was going to have the most expensive urine in the universe or that we had stumbled upon something that might keep me well. We raided the health food store. I bought natural curcumin (from turmeric) since it was reported to have cancer killing activity. In India, the stuff is even used on open wounds to heal them. I took green tea powder; aloe; milk thistle; coenzyme Q-10; an antioxidant vitamin; calcium tablets; vitamin c; selenium; and regular multivitamins. Each day I walked my neighborhood and drank a nutritional drink concoction with soy protein and some "green," such as alfalfa, to oxygenate my bloodstream.

I began what we called, "Food Chemo." Basically, the principle behind it was that I shouldn't eat anything unless it had anti-cancer properties. For instance, I could have a pizza now and then since the tomatoes, garlic, and low-fat Italian cheeses were alright. I didn't come close to processed foods, coldcuts, soda, or meals with preservatives or coloring. I increased my intake of cruciferous vegetables and citrus fruits.

The method used by several advanced cancer patients included not only something healthy going into their mouths, but a means of rinsing their systems: Enemas. I drew the line there. I heard of a woman who used coffee enemas to clean her body. Good for her and I hope that it works, but I increased my water consumption instead. It may pay to test your water supply. If you have any doubts about the cleanliness of the water then perhaps a filter is in order. During chemo., however, it is important to stay well hydrated in order to flush out the drugs. I simply continued to drink all of the time. The reasoning we had was that if the plumbing is crucial then I'll keep attempting to cleanse my system.

The discovery of herbal teas was a breakthrough for me. I had a tea for everything: Chamomile to relax me; there was a "sleepy time" mix for evenings; rosehip for extra vitamin C; and even a blend called "throat coat" which was quite soothing. I really got into the teas and it became a great way to increase fluids. Green tea tasted like dishwater to me so I added that in capsule form. There's a big selection of no-caffeine, herbal varieties and it actually bordered on being a hobby while I tried them. I figured that there was a reason why Peter Rabbit was given chamomile; some natural sedatives in tea were a help during such anxious days.

Wow was I altering my tastes! No more java with a muffin. I had my own teapot; I was talking to the birds and sipping tea; and I wore a wig. I knew that pure stress had aged me, but I seemed as if I'd become an old woman. Fortunately, my kids kept me grounded. Through their youthful outlook, I snapped out of the elderly woman feelings. Age is truly a state of mind.

Nutrition, however, affects the physical state. I wasn't losing too much weight and my new diet made me believe that I was participating in destroying the cancer. Whether you have cancer or not, I'd urge everyone to examine what they eat and to see if it's contributing to your health or not.

Sticking to my food chemo, my supplements, and

vitamins, I started to build up a routine. I derived some comfort from having a focus and from getting "order" back. My world had spun out of my control. I could at least determine what I put into my body. I was almost through my chemo and the decision about the bone marrow transplant had to be made. I was just beginning to have a schedule when my reality was challenged again.

Chapter VI

The Bone Marrow Transplant

My first impression of the bone marrow transplant description was that it was just science fiction. The decision whether to do it or not had been looming over me since hearing the oncologists all propose it. My husband behaved as if it would be another treatment step. I was scared out of my gourd after being diagnosed with cancer; the bone marrow transplant possibility hovered in my mind like a bad idea that wouldn't go away.

Closer to the decision time, my husband and I switched roles. I wanted to try the procedure so that I could feel as if I'd done everything that existed in 1997. What was more chemo at this point? Besides, the decision was out of my hands. My scans had to come out clean enough after chemo to be accepted for treatment. Not every medical center takes you because you want the treatment done. Furthermore, we had to verify that the procedure would be covered or mostly taken care of by insurance. Bills could reach over $100,000.

My husband was frustrated with the lack of scientific data on bone marrow transplants. There were several types and he voiced concerns about the procedure. He didn't know if I could withstand the treatment, especially after the high dose chemotherapy I'd already taken. There was a mortality rate associated with it; granted, it wasn't high, but there was a much greater risk than standard chemotherapy. What was more maddening was that each institution appeared to have its own bone marrow transplant approach. There were protocols that were followed that differed in the drugs used, too. On the west coast, a soy diet was part of the protocol at one hospital. The University of Pennsylvania was world-class in cutting edge technology and treatments, but it offered only a limited number of protocols.

In theory, we wanted to stay with whatever would keep my immune system intact. We started more information and advice gathering. I met a woman who'd had a transplant. She had been cancer free for 18 months, but now the cancer was in her bones. Another woman I spoke with had been fine for five years. My oncologist urged me to have the procedure. He admitted that, in his own practice, the numbers were about even--with maybe a slight edge in survival to those who'd undergone the treatment.

Meanwhile, my uncle was dying of lung cancer. I didn't wish to think of hospitals or treatments. After almost six months of chemo or twelve hits of the poison, we had another consultation at the University of Pennsylvania. All the risks were outlined. The process was explained: A pulmonary function test would be needed; a heart test; scans; and blood work had to be done. A bone marrow biopsy was critical to see if the marrow looked clean after all of the chemotherapy. If I elected to go ahead, a decision was required regarding whether or not my cancer would be viewed as metastatic. If not, I could follow a protocol that was slightly less severe than others. The bone marrow transplant was actually at a point where your own marrow or stem cells could be collected. The concept was that your cells would be harvested and stored, but your body would be bombarded for several days with strong chemo agents. The stored cells would then be reimplanted into your body. My oncologist's analogy summed it up: "It's what we do with a computer when you push the restart button; the doctors are trying to 'reboot' your body."

How do I know if my cells will be clean enough? Can the doctors check the cells or clean them before they're transplanted back into you? Apparently, some centers do "purge" the cells, but Penn's method was based on a store and then transplant process. To have the transplant, I would also need two operations. A catheter had to be inserted so I could be hooked up to a device, which was like a dialysis machine, and the cells could be collected. It would take time for surgery and then several days of commuting to Philadelphia for the stem cell collection. Another operation, upon admission to the hospital, would put a Hickman catheter into my body for delivering the chemo straight into my veins. The Hickman could also be used for blood transfusions, blood testing, and more. With any luck, the hospital stay would be from 21 days to a month.

We were on information overload again. My head was spinning. Once more, instincts took over. I liked the doctor at Penn and she was straightforward. No one was distributing great hope, but at least they weren't saying that it wasn't worth doing. My parents were careful not to influence our decision, but once it was made, they visibly sighed with relief. I had concluded that anecdotal evidence was more crucial to me than scientific data. There were women walking around who'd been through the procedure and that was enough for now.

One point on cancer treatments: Don't second guess them. Once you've made your choices, you have to believe that they will help you. I reminded myself of that reasoning as my lips tingled and Tums were popped into my mouth while I was attached to the cold, metal, stem cell collection machine. My cells were being harvested. It was late December and we hadn't had much holiday cheer. My admission date was early January. I was paranoid because I wouldn't be allowed in if I had a cold.

I sneaked out of the house with my husband around 5:00 am one morning. We had been told to report in for my catheter surgery by 6:30 am and to be prepared to wait. The hospital provides a small waiting room with cozy chairs and a television set. An orderly with a clipboard called my name and my day began. The surgery went well. I sat for about six hours in the post operative area; my arrival onto the bone marrow unit floor was delayed due to overcrowding. I was brought to another waiting space, but it was going on over eight hours and I still didn't have a room. When finally provided with a bed, I found out that I had another patient next to me. She was not in good shape. I tried to speak with her, but soon realized that she did not want to communicate.

My chemo regimen began and we were assured that a different room would be prepared in a few days. When the vomiting started, it didn't let up. I hadn't been nauseous during the first day of the drugs so I had been hoping that I'd escape the throwing up. By the time I had my own room, I was sick several times a day for weeks on end. My husband stayed with me day and night. I could not have seen any light at the end of the tunnel without him.

Blood transfusions and platelet transfusions were all a necessary part of the treatment. My cell counts were now down to nothing. I had no immunity. The nurses wore face masks and I feared infection. I was so vulnerable that germs could literally kill me.

During a particularly fun afternoon of vomiting non-stop and having the runs, we were notified that our car had been robbed in the Penn parking garage. While my husband attended to the matter, a nurse called for more potassium. A resident took care of the orders. I had so many different substances dripping into me that I lost track of them. When my husband returned from consulting with the campus police, he informed me that the robbers had been caught and our property had been recovered. A few days earlier, a huge chunk of concrete had fallen on top of our car. The weather had been freezing, then warm, and back to frosty January days. A piece of the garage flooring on the level above our car had dropped below. I laughed hysterically at both incidents and my husband worried about my mental state.

The doctor on duty and his assistant made evening rounds. I was known as the "vomit queen" since they usually found me in that activity. The time was approaching to have the cells transplanted back into me. It was like being in a Star Trek episode. The most nerve-wracking wait was upon us. We had to hope that my body would "come back." The whole idea of the procedure is that you are taken almost to the point of death and then, hopefully, restored all "clean."

When my blood counts had reached an acceptable level, I was allowed to return home and to have visiting nurse care. The Hickman catheter had to be rinsed with solutions to prevent infection. I had injections to boost my cell counts. Have you seen any Frankenstein movies? I could not have been more amazed and awed by the process. Within a week of lying in my own bed, I went to Penn for a check-up on my own steam.

Someday, my friend was fond of telling me, society will look back on what was done to cancer patients and shudder with horror. Looking back on the use of leeches seems mild compared with chemotherapy and surgery. The other "slash and burn" methods will be viewed as equally archaic. Cancer is complicated. It's also not just one disease. I believe that it will take several methods to control it and my personal frustration is that I don't see an interdisciplinary approach being used. We may require immunologists, engineers, and creative problem solving scientists, to work as a team in oncological research. Today, the field is loaded with medical doctors and biologists who have made wonderful contributions, but whose behavior is still territorial. Ideas must be shared across many disciplines.

Remarkably, I was in my local oncologist's office by mid-February. I had plenty of time to think about the cancer industry and the answers that were desperately needed. Although I was worn out, I was glad that I had tried the stem cell/bone marrow treatment. It was the biggest hurdle in my schedule and I had just jumped it. Radiation sounded like a piece of cake in comparison.

Although I hadn't looked as if I'd be a candidate for tamoxifen, my oncologist wrote a prescription for it. He explained that it was worth it for a woman of my age and with my situation. I continued with regular check-ups at Penn. I began walking again. I took my herbs and vitamins. Routines were forming in my life. By March, though, I hoped to be prepared for my radiation treatments.

Chapter VII

Radiation and Inspiration

One of my most bizarre dreams was about my catheter. An unshaven resident, who looked like a zombie, had tugged on my catheter tubes to remove them. For a Hickman catheter, an incision is made near the collarbone and one shoulder. Plastic lines are stuffed into the body and the whole contraption extends from a tube coming out of a hole in the chest. To prevent ripping myself open, a safety pin on some gauze secured the device to my hospital gown.

I dreamed that endless amounts of tubing were pulled from me. The resident didn't care that he had piles of the plastic at his feet. While the tubes kept coming, I had a sudden flow of liquid down my legs. Perhaps I was remembering the bodily fluids that were a part of the bone marrow transplant. You lose your dignity quickly in hospitals.

I awoke and, with relief, ran my fingers over the scars

where the catheter had been. I stayed in bed staring blankly at the alarm clock, unable to move, and not ready to get dressed. Today was my appointment with the radiologist, yet it wasn't a big deal to me. I had been fighting a feeling of resignation. It had been almost a year since I was diagnosed and I'd put my body through one medical hell after another.

My husband had taken time off from work to stay with me in the hospital. The radiation treatment could be done at a local hospital about 30 minutes away. I was determined to drive myself to the treatments. It was the "home stretch" of treatments, maybe six weeks of radiation, and I had to tackle it.

The radiologist was a young, empathetic woman who carefully outlined the game plan. I'd have to return for some tattoos and "blocks" so they could set the equipment up properly for me. The radiologist also informed me that she had a colleague who'd founded the "Living Beyond Breast Cancer," organization. The group provided helplines and offered conferences on a variety of subjects. One of the nurse-technicians was a breast cancer survivor herself. The radiologist's next words floored me, though: "Of course,

I'm regarding you as a disease-free patient at the moment so the radiation is really a preventative measure." Here was a real, live medical doctor who thought I was recovering from cancer!

"You think that it's medically possible for a person in my high-risk category to stay alright?" I asked wonderingly.

All through my treatments, the odds of lasting had seemed so against me. It was strong medicine to have the doctor smile and say, "Yes, it's possible."

After that interview, I didn't care what they did to me. There was a cold table and I couldn't move. The nurses were kind and recommended various ointments for burns. I barely heard them. I was still absorbing the idea that I could maybe beat the disease. Naturally, I had tried to remain positive and believe in a good outcome, but to have a doctor act as the radiologist had was music to my soul.

My skin became raw and then it was cooked after a month. Burned and tired, I told myself that there was only a little more to endure. Meanwhile, I was sick of my wig, but thrilled to notice the teeniest stubble forming underneath it. I'd lost eyebrows and eyelashes from the chemo which were still gone. At least my hair was returning.

Every weekday I commuted to the hospital. The kids went off to school; my husband to work; and I drove to my unusual job: Lying totally still and being zapped. Toward the last days of the treatment, my mother visited us and she drove me to the hospital. My burns, especially under my arm, made gripping the steering wheel tough.

Although my body burned, my mouth sores from chemo were almost all healed. To test my gums, I sampled some salsa. I was also starting to put on some weight. More importantly, I became interested in the world around me again. I chose a new route home from the hospital each week. Afterall, we'd barely become familiar with our region when I was put out of commission.

I still thought about cancer fifty million times a day. Every twinge, each joint pain, or a headache, created anxiety: Did it mean that the cancer was back? Taking Tamoxifen reminded me of my circumstances, too. My oncologist had assured me that, one day, it would be like brushing my teeth--totally automatic. At the time, I bit back a sarcastic reply. Like brushing teeth? Impossible. Remember when there were records and the needle got stuck in a groove of a song? My mind played over and over the tune that I was in a high risk for recurrence group.

By April of 1997, I had to admit that my oncologist was right. I only thought of cancer thirty million times a day now and I popped those little Tamoxifen pills, morning and night, as if they were TicTacs.

When radiation was over, several scans were scheduled. The nurse setting up the chest X-ray had asked me to place two stickers over my nipples. When I said that I didn't have any, she was aghast. With a pitying look, she arranged for the rest of my tests.

Spring is my favorite season. That particular spring, I inhaled deeply on my walks and I was flooded with gratitude to be alive. By May, it was tempting to burn my wig. I ripped it off and started to wear baseball caps over my ultra short hair, instead. My immune system was trying to repair itself. I came down with a nasty sinus infection. Later, I thought that my radiation burns had returned from being in the warm air. My skin hurt, but I also had terrible pains on my back. It turned out that I had shingles! The radiologist who examined my welts reassured me that having shingles "portend nothing." I was worried, though, that I was going downhill.

By summer, the kids were enjoying being on a swimteam and I was happy to sit in the shade and watch them. The kids experienced their old activities with me chaffeuring them as before. It was as if we'd all been in some gruesome time warp. For me, it was also odd being thrown in the company of so many healthy people again.

One afternoon I had lunch with the woman who'd had a bone marrow transplant and a recurrence in her bones. The cancer was still in her leg, but the latest scan showed that it hadn't spread. She told me a wonderful tale about seeing a rainbow and how she realized that she must be fine. I was happy for her peace of mind and wondered how one achieved the ability to erase doubts. She managed to live for another few years, but she died recently. We had exchanged cards; the kind that assure someone that you're thinking of them. A few weeks later, I saw her picture on the obituary page.

Several other women were in touch with me when they were diagnosed with breast cancer. Most of them were in their thirties with children. Breast cancer is an epidemic. These women knew others in various stages of the disease and they were waiting for their pathology reports. The women had distinct personalities: One relied entirely upon her faith; the other depended on pills. I tried to keep their spirits up. I mused that I was a case of the "blind leading the blind." The religious woman accepted the news that one lymph node was positive. She planned to visit a shrine and then consider doing a mastectomy. The other woman had no lymph node involvement and didn't require chemotherapy. Her doctor expected her to do well. She blurted out to me, "How do you stand your situation?"

With cancer, there always seemed to be someone who was worse off than me and I also knew that you couldn't take anything for granted: Some women who were supposed to be fine, just weren't and others with a terrible prognosis were still kicking. More women called. Their friends had urged them to talk to me. One woman was in her sixties; another had tumors which had spread to her back but they were responding to treatment; one woman had a relative dying of the disease. A courageous woman with breast cancer had been writing a weekly column for a local newspaper. I never met her but I admired her efforts to call attention to the disease. She died without reaching 30.

To my surprise, I had my own "rainbow" story. On a gorgeous, sunny afternoon, a neighbor stopped by to pick up her child who'd been playing soccer with my son. We chatted for a few minutes together while the boys finished their game in our yard. My neighbor finally asked how I was doing. A few clouds blocked the sun and I replied, "We're keeping our fingers crossed. I just wish that someone could guarantee that it'll be alright."

At that moment, a rainbow appeared. Stunned, the boys dropped their soccer balls. "Hey a rainbow!" they shouted in excitement, "but there isn't a sign of any rain."

Within seconds, the rainbow disappeared as fast as it had arrived. My neighbor chuckled uncomfortably, "That was weird, wasn't it?"

Was I developing a new spirituality? Was the rainbow a good signal? Was I so desperate? I just knew that I'd never be the same person and yet I was still "me." I didn't know what to make of the incident.

I was an object of curiosity to many people. There was a vague awareness that I'd been through something awful. I fended off a lot of well-meaning but stupid comments. I was never sure how to answer the questions. I didn't want to jinx anything by saying I was fine. The next person who said, "You're cured, right?" was going to get punched.

I was torn between searching for inspiration or researching contingency plans. Rainbows were beautiful, but my brain demanded scientific action. What was this "angiogenesis" I'd heard about on the news? Should I be keeping up with any advances? What about preventing a recurrence: Why weren't there any guidelines about what to do--should I adopt a special lifestyle?

By the time I saw my oncologist for a check-up, it was early summer and I was depressed. Did I even have a future? I never lost sight of being thrilled to be among the living, but I sensed that I was in a sort of limbo. I certainly didn't want to be whining when I was so lucky to be around. My existence, however, had centered on doctor visits and treatments for a year. It had all stopped cold-turkey. My oncologist was familiar with the condition. I joked that it was almost like having postpartum depression. He pointed out that I just required some weaning from him. He wanted me to get on with my life. We then had the promised guitar jam.

In the following weeks, I did mental exercises. If you

have a 15% chance of being alive, that means: In a room of 100 people, 15 would still be standing. Why couldn't I be one of those 15? Rather than worry about a recurrence, why not think of the poor souls who've been suddenly struck down without warning? What about the travelers on TWA Flight 800? What if you're hit by a truck?

I also concentrated on the kids and my husband. Food shopping even seemed fun since I was back doing it for my family. We decided, though, that a change in scene was in order. Hesitant to plan any vacation before, we browsed the papers to check if there were any good airfares. For ages we'd talked of going out west to the Grand Tetons and Yellowstone, one day. The famous "one day" we'd all mentioned became the "why not now?" plan.

Chapter VIII

Yellowstone Park and Al Gore

In keeping with my back-to-nature feelings and our goal to take the kids out west, we came up with a vacation: Fly to Salt Lake City, rent a car, see some of Utah, Wyoming, Montana, and Idaho. It was August and we were where the deer and the antelope play.

With a Holiday Inn as a base, we explored Salt Lake City. To my delight, it was a smoke-free city. We toured Temple Square and visited the geneaology center of the Mormons. Piling into the rental car, we traveled to the Great Salt Lake. A state park on an island of the lake allowed us to have our first view of buffalo. At one of the lake's beaches, we took off our socks and shoes and waded into the shallow waters. A serenity I hadn't felt in a long time stole over me. As a kid, the ocean had had the same mystical power to lull me into another world. The Great Salt Lake gave me some of the same peace.

We journeyed off the beaten path through Logan, Utah and into a small corner of Idaho called "Bear Lake." Markers reminded us of covered wagon trails and settlers who'd risked their lives to head west. The mountains were similar to those in Iceland: Bold, treeless, colorful sand monuments that could reduce your problems to nothing. We pressed on to Jackson Hole, Wyoming, past the mighty Snake River. The landscape was dramatic and powerful.

We spotted a black bear in the Tetons and made our way leisurely through Yellowstone. I had made reservations in a river lodge up in Gardiner, Montana, a small town near the north entrance of the park. We were planning on making several forays into Yellowstone from the less crowded north. A moose jumped in front of the car. The kids squealed. We spotted bison in the distance. We pulled into Gardiner and were pleased with the accommodations. We had a little kitchenette so we were set to explore the town and raid a grocery store.

Our first evening there was peaceful. We were on the banks of the Yellowstone River, light years away from hospitals or intravenous equipment. My husband bought a fishing permit and some rods. The following day we found an isolated fishing spot; toured Mammoth Hot Springs; and explored. I surprised myself that I had the stamina to climb some small hills.

An item in the park newspaper reported that the 125th anniversary of Yellowstone was approaching and that a ceremony would be held in the park. Vice President Al Gore was expected to visit and to be the keynote speaker. We inquired about the event at the visitor center and learned that we could attend. I had always been impressed with Al Gore and had voted for him. He and President Clinton had accomplished so much for families. My aunt was able to use the "family leave act" in order to be with my uncle when he was dying. I explained to our children that, if we were lucky, perhaps we'd get a glimpse of Al Gore.

One of my daughters and I decided to pass on another fishing expedition and we strolled into Gardiner. We stopped in a boutique selling Montana sweatshirts with moose pictures. The boutique owner struck up a conversation with us and then she admitted that she'd had quite a morning. The secret service had been all over her place with dogs sniffing across the old wooden floors. Yes, the vice president was staying in Gardiner.

"Those Washington folk think we're crazy here in Montana," she confided in us. "Ever since the Freemen and well, the Unabomber, you know."

I told her that we were hoping to be at the park anniversary ceremony. She volunteered to call some buddies and find out how we could attend the event since security was so tight. She had learned that a bus would be leaving Gardiner in the morning and that no one would be allowed to drive their own vehicle to Mammoth Hot Springs. If we wanted to be on the bus, we had to show up at the town's school.

With a handful of informed locals, we climbed aboard the bus and we were soon deposited near a roped off area. We saw the visitor center; the whole area was swarming with agents. Our cameras were checked by asking us to shoot a picture. Once we passed through the security inspectors, we noticed a podium that was set up. The sound system was being tested. Rows of chairs, for about 50 special guests, were arranged in front of the podium and a military band was warming up nearby. Ropes defined where the rest of us could stand and they also marked an "entrance" for the dignitaries arriving by car. We positioned ourselves behind the ropes ready to watch for the vips arriving. Along with Vice President Gore, the Secretary of the Interior, Bruce Babbitt, was expected, accompanied by Montana Senator Max Baucus.

Our kids had seen "Men in Black" and they stared, awestruck, at Will Smith lookalikes. Park rangers mingled with big men in dark sunglasses. We waited. We'd been among the first to take up a position. More people started filling the seats or joining us behind the ropes. Some of the guests were escorted to specific chairs. A press van pulled up and journalists poured out. We stood in the hot sun patiently. After my radiation treatments, I took precautions. I was self-conscious with my super short hair and sunhat. It was fine with me to blend into a crowd and just enjoy the day.

To our astonishment, moments before the celebration was due to begin, a park ranger approached us. "Would you like seats?" he asked. We nodded affirmatively. "Follow me."

We would have been thrilled to have anything to sit on in the back row. In amazement, we realized that the ranger was showing us to the front seats! We never knew if there had been a cancellation by someone's party; whether the speech, which included references to the next generation's care of the park, called for some children to be present; whether we'd been checked out and found to be a safe family to have there; or if it was sheer dumb luck. There we were, directly opposite the podium, only a few feet from the Vice President of the United States of America.

My husband had recently become an American citizen. He was as awestruck as we were to find ourselves in the front row. My son didn't move a muscle. He had noticed a tall man, with his arms crossed like a genie, who looked as if he could chop you in two with a stare. The girls behaved like young ladies and politely listened to the talks.

A local woman was given the honor of introducing Al Gore. She mistakenly called him "President Gore." He graciously explained that the lady was technically correct because he was the president of the senate. He put her at ease and elicited a chuckle from the crowd. It was a kind-hearted gesture and one in keeping with my impression of the man.

I didn't have a great grip on reality after all I'd been doing. As we recognized Yellowstone's anniversary, I thought that life was truly remarkable. I had hoped to find some healing possible on my trip. I was shown reminders of nature's ability to survive. Everywhere around me: Yellowstone's example was the epitome of learning to adapt and go on. Terrible forest fires which once had destroyed huge sections of the park now had life in them again. From the microbes in the hot springs to the wolves returning to the lands, the message was one of rebirth.

When the speeches ended, another shock was in store. Al Gore was leaving the podium and shaking hands with everyone in the front row. People were mumbling that it was a pleasure to meet him or just bowing their heads in greeting. I don't know what possessed me. I had wanted to thank Al Gore for a long time for caring about the environment. I'd always believed that pollution had played a role in causing my cancer. When the vice president stood before me, I quickly said, "I have breast cancer and I'd like to thank you for your efforts on the environment..."

I don't remember what else was expressed except that then I was gripped in a bear hug. My sunhat was being knocked off by the embrace and I reached up to fix it. I had such a tiny bit of hair, but large tears came to my eyes. Al

Gore's sincerity about my situation and his genuine warmth had me choked up. I believe that he really cared.

The other politicians had good records on environmental issues and they were obviously curious about my identity. I repeated similar words about being grateful to them for protecting the environment. They weren't interested in me, probably because I wasn't famous. With polite detachment, they moved down the row and soon exited the area. I wondered immediately if I'd done the right thing: To use the opportunity to communicate with the vice president instead of giving a perfunctory few words. What I did came straight from the heart, though. I'd always admired Al Gore and now I was extremely impressed with him. He'd never know, however, how much his response meant to me.

We watched coverage of the day's event from our river lodge rooms. One CNN reporter gave such a negative view of Yellowstone that my family wanted to protest to the network. All of us are not only defenders of the park, but we won't hear a single comment against Al Gore. The jaded journalists who didn't find cause for celebration were to be pitied, we concluded.

When we departed Gardiner, we headed toward Craters

of the Moon, Idaho. We were sometimes the only car on the road as we traveled past miles of old, barren, lava beds. The Craters of the Moon region was fascinating and we enjoyed exploring it. We then stayed in Pocatello, Idaho for the night, but pushed on to Salt Lake City the next morning. Our flight to Philadelphia had the kids surrounded by Mormon missionaries. We chatted during the trip and learned about their assignments. Refreshed, recharged, and reunited with our dog, we came home.

Chapter IX

Reflections With A Sword Over the Head

Cancer is not just a disease; it's an industry. Millions of dollars go into the salaries of doctors and the running of institutions. If I could wave a wand, I'd create a dream team for cancer research. My dream team would operate in a dream world. Public and private money would stream together with the objective of finding a cure. There's too much job security in oncology. Every day, more cancer cases are diagnosed. In the hustle and bustle of administering standard treatments, no united effort is being made. Researchers work in secret and guard their advances. When findings are published, some colleagues ridicule the results. The fellow who came up with the angiogenesis theories, developed them about 20 years ago.

One woman is certain that breast cancer has been put on the back burner because we don't have many CEOs with the illness. It's easy to become very cynical. Sometimes when

I'm trying to wrestle with one of the paper medical gowns before a check-up, I think about how little progress has been made for women. As I hope that my lymph nodes are behaving, I resent that there isn't a bigger push to provide new cancer treatments.

It is one year since my bone marrow transplant. Twelve months, fifty two weeks, 365 days, and I'm actually here. For the first time, I can write again. My doctor visits and scan appointments sprinkle the calendar, but I'm with my family. I have succeeded in living one day at a time.

I used to be the type of person who liked projecting ahead into the future. Now I cannot afford to think that way. Today is just another day to pack a lot of living into and to share with those I love. I've been able to change and stay more in the present. Sometimes it's difficult. I get a lump in my throat when someone speaks of attending their child's graduation, an occasion still years away. I don't know what the future will bring, but I can only keep hoping. For some cancer patients, it's called "having a sword over your head." Our language provides many descriptive manners to say the same thing, such as: "Waiting for the other shoe to drop." I'm not sure if another expression, "time heals" is always correct, but I do think that time provides a chance to adjust.

I got my first bi-focals the other day. My hair has lost the "Harpo Marx" style that seems to occur after chemo affects it. I take my herbs, supplements, and stick to my food-chemo diet. Walking is part of my daily routine. I'm "holding my breath," but becoming a little more relaxed about doing so. Once in a while, I have questions.

My left arm had stiffened up on me. For a long time I'd worried about getting lymphodema or swelling of the arm after surgery. When I had trouble lifting my arm over my head, I thought that I'd better call the surgeon's office. I mainly wanted to ascertain if what I was experiencing was normal or not. Thanks to war stories from other breast cancer patients, I'd heard of "tissues tightening" within their arms. Was that what I was having?

Too lazy to locate the business card from my surgeon's office, I called information for the phone number. I dialed the number and a nurse answered my call: "How long ago did you have surgery?"

"In the spring of '96," I said.

She added, "That long ago?!"

I explained to her that my arm was hurting.

"Your arm?" she queried in surprise.

"Yes."

"Are you sure it's your arm?"

"Of course," I replied. "I just wondered if it's normal for my arm to be bothering me now and if you knew why it could be..."

"Jesus, just a minute!"

I heard some whispering in the background. A different woman jumped on the line. "Can I help you?" she asked defensively.

Once more I stated my situation and posed my question. The only difference this time was that I mentioned breast cancer.

"Breast cancer?! Oh, wait a sec., breast cancer? You probably want Dr. X, the surgeon!"

"Isn't this his office?" I groaned.

"Well, yes. This is Dr. X's office, but this Dr. X is a periodontist."

I sighed. The computerized phone information service had spit out the number of a guy who operated on gums! No wonder they were so horrified when I complained about my arm.

Eventually I was connected with the correct Dr. X and I received word that my arm was probably going through some tissue tightening. A few weeks later, the problem was gone.

In the stress reduction department, getting back to regular routines was the best help. I rely on my herb teas, cozy times, and I try to stay happy. I don't have anything to do with people who get me down. I also haven't graduated from comedies to other types of films, yet. While my kids saw "Titanic," I sat through "Mouse Hunt" in the same theater complex!

My blood counts are still low. I suppose that I'm operating with less white cells than most of society, but I'm getting stronger. I take common-sense precautions; it's easy to wipe off the shopping cart handle so I watch out for germs.

There are days which cause philosophical moods. I've discovered that among the women survivors, many put themselves last in the family pecking order. They didn't take as much care of themselves as they did their spouses and/or children. Breast cancer: A lifestyle disease. The phrase haunts me. Our lives must be examined. We must be aware of our habits, our water, our foods, and even the air we breathe.

I have more questions than answers about my illness. We're told that new treatments are on the horizon. Like a desert mirage, the image moves away when we get closer. There are leads, but currently nothing I could depend upon should the cancer spread. I worry about my children and wonder if they're at a greater risk of coming down with cancer.

It has been a wild journey. Like Alice in Wonderland, only in a medical hell, it feels as if I've been on the other side of a looking glass. The trip back is one that I hope takes an extremely long time to complete. Meanwhile, descriptions such as "dull" and "boring" have become wonderful words to me. How shall I describe my existence after being treated for an advanced case of breast cancer? Uneventful, I hope.

Chapter X

A Resource List

Since I strongly recall my lack of an attention span and the need to have immediate information, I've compiled a resource list for the Internet. Most doctor offices can provide standard mail addresses for organizations and agencies which deal with cancer. I recommend, however, the following sites:

OncoLink-Breast Cancer

http://www.oncolink.upenn.edu/disease/breast

Breast CancerInfo.Com

http://www.breastcancerinfo.com

National Alliance of Breast Cancer Organizations

http://www.nabco.org

Y-ME National Breast Cancer Organization
http://www.y-me.org

Breast Cancer Network--American Cancer Society
http://www.cancer.org/bcn/brmenu.html

CancerNet (National Cancer Institute)
http://cancernet.nci.nih.gov

Resources (Cont.)

Doctor's Guide to Breast Cancer Information &
    Resources
http://www.psigroup.com/breastcancer.htm

National Breast Cancer Coalition
http://www.natibcc.org

National Action Plan on Breast Cancer
http://www.napbc.org

The Susan G. Komen Breast Cancer Foundation

http://www.breastcancerinfo.com

American Cancer Society

http://www.cancer.org

Cancer Care, Inc.

http://www.cancercareinc.org

Many regions have their own breast cancer information groups. It is worth asking about them. There are also some other specialized sites which cover breast cancer:

National Asian Women's Health Organization

http://www.nawho.org

Native American Program of Excellence at the AMC
    Cancer
Research Center

http://www.aclin.org/code/nac

National Hispanic Leadership Initiative on Cancer:
    En

Accion/Baylor College of Medicine

http://cccr.bcm.tmc.edu/enaccion/

Hadassah

http://www.hadassah.org

About the Author

V.S. Brynn is the author's pen name. She is a free-lance writer and mother of three children. She holds a master's degree in communication and has worked as a vice president of communication; director of public relations; and as a journalist. The author also has extensive experience as an educational and an intercultural consultant. Having held top positions in community organizations, she is still active in cross-cultural causes. Her husband is from Reykjavik, Iceland.

www.ingramcontent.com/pod-product-compliance
Lightning Source LLC
Chambersburg PA
CBHW050403290526
45786CB00003B/1103